MAGNIFIER

THE COLORADO PRIZE FOR POETRY

Strike Anywhere, by Dean Young
selected by Charles Simic, 1995

Summer Mystagogia, by Bruce Beasley
selected by Charles Wright, 1996

The Thicket Daybreak, by Catherine Webster
selected by Jane Miller, 1997

Palma Cathedral, by Michael White
selected by Mark Strand, 1998

Popular Music, by Stephen Burt
selected by Jorie Graham, 1999

Design, by Sally Keith
selected by Allen Grossman, 2000

A Summer Evening, by Geoffrey Nutter
selected by Jorie Graham, 2001

Chemical Wedding, by Robyn Ewing
selected by Fanny Howe, 2002

Goldbeater's Skin, by G. C. Waldrep
selected by Donald Revell, 2003

Whethering, by Rusty Morrison
selected by Forrest Gander, 2004

Frayed escort, by Karen Garthe
selected by Cal Bedient, 2005

Carrier Wave, by Jaswinder Bolina
selected by Lyn Hejinian, 2006

Brenda Is in the Room and Other Poems,
by Craig Morgan Teicher
selected by Paul Hoover, 2007

One Sun Storm, by Endi Bogue Hartigan
selected by Martha Ronk, 2008

The Lesser Fields, by Rob Schlegel
selected by James Longenbach, 2009

Annulments, by Zach Savich
selected by Donald Revell, 2010

Scared Text, by Eric Baus
selected by Cole Swensen, 2011

Family System, by Jack Christian
selected by Elizabeth Willis, 2012

Intimacy, by Catherine Imbriglio
selected by Stephen Burt, 2013

Supplice, by T. Zachary Cotler
selected by Claudia Keelan, 2014

The Business, by Stephanie Lenox
selected by Laura Kasischke, 2015

Exit Theater, by Mike Lala
selected by Tyrone Williams, 2016

Instead of Dying, by Lauren Haldeman
selected by Susan Howe, 2017

The Owl Was a Baker's Daughter,
by Gillian Cummings
selected by John Yau, 2018

Magnifier, by Brandon Krieg
selected by Kazim Ali, 2019

MAGNIFIER

poems

BRANDON KRIEG

The Center for Literary Publishing
Colorado State University

For information about permission to reproduce
selections from this book, write to
The Center for Literary Publishing
attn: Permissions
9105 Campus Delivery
Colorado State University
Fort Collins, Colorado 80523-9105.

Printed in the United States of America.

Library of Congress Cataloging-in-Publication Data

Names: Krieg, Brandon, author.
Title: Magnifier : poems / Brandon Krieg.
Description: Fort Collins, Colorado : The Center for Literary Publishing,
   [2019]
Identifiers: LCCN 2019035067 (print) | LCCN 2019035068 (ebook) |
ISBN 9781885635693 (paperback) | ISBN 9781885635709 (ebook)
Subjects: LCGFT: Poetry.
Classification: LCC PS3611.R53 A6 2019 (print) | LCC PS3611.R53 (ebook) |
   DDC 881/.6--dc23
LC record available at https://lccn.loc.gov/2019035067
LC ebook record available at https://lccn.loc.gov/2019035068

The paper used in this book meets the minimum requirements of the
American National Standard for Information Sciences-Permanence of Paper
for Printed Library Materials, ANSI Z39.48-1984.

1 2 3 4 5   23 22 21 20 19

Let Fig, house of Fig rejoice with Fleawort. The Lord magnify the idea of Smart singing hymns on this day. . . .

Christopher Smart, *Jubilate Agno*

In the autumn the leaves fall to the ground, accumulate in sodden layers, and begin the slow process of becoming one with the soil. In this they are aided by the toil of the earthworms, who feed in the leaf litter, for elm leaves are among their favorite foods. In feeding on the leaves the worms also swallow the insecticide, accumulating and concentrating it in their bodies. . . . Undoubtedly some of the earthworms themselves succumb, but others survive to become "biological magnifiers" of the poison.

Rachel Carson, *Silent Spring*

CONTENTS

FOUR

ONE

Magnifier

Fallen Osage orange smells
like boards at a construction site
I used to climb through
stealing nails I didn't need
The adults laughed at the scream
of lobsters in the pot
Bump stocks and bibles
said the wind in the trees
Your rewards will be many:
hedge funds and hegemony
I added that last part
after fancy college
Grades tattooed on my ankle
Even the air is ranked
like a snack or a scripture
Maybe you see me as
a black pearl suddenly valuable
I'm the roach in the knife drawer
wearing a mask of white mold
engorged with atrazine
sipped from a dew-bead
my gaze snowed-out
like a robbed carved god
on display for donors
Soon I'll donate my body
to popular culture
to eat me and absorb
these parts per million—
what's left of afternoons
by the spillway under the interstate
taking hit after hit
of oceanic feeling

Comedy of Mirrors

Cinema on the hill: a few frames of rain
without human story.

Born, and the search already ended.

These rampant blackberries introduced
for profit on three taxonomic axes,

this volcanic ash a year in the news cycle
despite so few bodies.

She incredulous: *The falls are left on at night?*

*

And saw from there cloud-shadows on the reefs
where no clouds were, dark shapes perhaps

decommissioned
tanks sunk

to shelter lingcod, cabezon—a discoverable use
waits to absorb each form;
a man dances

behind a signboard as cars pass; after interval n
the program repeats the landscape features:

And saw from there this huge oxidized sun thread the eye
of the overpasses, aware again

as if of a beeping in the house
whose source cannot be found.

*

Like Lost Childhood still wandering the Management Area—

clearcuts, fireweed, fin-clipped steelhead
rebuffed by spillways,

come to rest in an ovoid pool under the structure
erected at the meridian of the fourth and fifth ice advances,

in the center of the salt marshes,
in the center of the brackish marshes,
in the proscenium

whose columns are a succession of ice cores dissolving,
overawing the dams, the audience
wears the masks:

neither cosmic nor tragic but comfortable with the holes cut
for screen's light to access the eyes.

*

And stood under the sulfur flares
and saw from that height to where the subdivision repeats,

remembering the father and the mother
pouring syrups into pools,

the children gazing into the pools.

*

Hot donuts, fried prawns, cold fishwater
swept into drains, the smells

of human breath and low-tide seaweed,
he found a bench under scaffolded totems in a park
above the highway viaduct, watched
containerships haul lost seasons—

Thai rice   Bolivian lithium—

to the orange waiting cranes.

*

And in that city with mountains on either side
she read *Borrowed Love Poems* to him,
and Rilke's letters,
and he kissed the mole beneath her breast:

a pebble among pebbles picked

from the riverbed of childhood, where the hook-jawed gods
washed from sex up onto the shore rocks dead.

And saw from there the source

of the red light on the walls of her tiny studio:
the radio tower on the hill.

And listened to the uncanny broadcast
picked up by her record player as it played:

Bach descending the spiral staircase into
an Iranian centrifuge.

*

And the music stopped, and the dancers who swayed against each other
long after it stopped
stopped too.

Rilke had been paraphrased
for the vows, and *Borrowed Love Poems* read
under the florist's wire trellis.

He stared into the camera thinking
I will see this picture of myself many years from now

staring into the camera thinking
I will see this picture of myself many years from now.

On this screen it has happened,
the life that seemed my own like a mirror or a garden;

it is a mirror held up to a mirror, a garden held up to a garden;
it belongs to neither the beholder nor the rain.

In Case of Loss

repeat what you can
commute five miles
dismantle the set
rest your buzzed head
against the arch of the storm
your cause is this green
of light in new leaves
petition the pollen
for thousandfold returns
vineyards and pergolas
enduring enemies
make your heart push
blood through your ears
submerged in a tub
tear the certificate
breathe on the glass
see what belief is
the bloody feathers
consult the dry canyons
whose rivers now reign
on thrones behind dams
the stars are reactors
some conglomerate will tap
you won't be consulted
return to ritual
that park always empty
sit under scaffolding
like sparrows or squirrels
neither in nor out
kneel down with your animal
a heartbeat is strange
in any container
step out of the soundtrack

into pine smell and pismires
raying out from a center
return to the verse
marked by another
read it with feeling
to a wall peeling layers
are you a user with access
then enter the portal
sit and say nothing
to a child on the steps
the boardwalks the ice creams
the brainless full summer
knocked down by waves
shell bits in teeth
the hands extended
must be gripped each in turn
placeholder to placeholder
peel off the sticker
put away the pictures
unplug the devices
throw her lock on the eggshells
in the bag at the curb
petition the snows
coming from nowhere
they may bring news
meet her that January
as Physics allows
meet her that June
the pool where crabs scatter
from cleaning the machinery
of the music she loved
each wave rocks it slightly
answer the waves
coming from shores
of nowhere with questions
You lovers you prophets
which silence is yours?

The Lover in Winter Plaineth

Machines grind wind's fangs
to flour. Piles heap

on the outskirts. I cannot see
to the edge. I creep

again to my niche. I sleep,
fingers triggered
from touching the keys.

Alders wave the river smell
into the hangar. I kneel again to scrape
gilt from illuminations

for re-use. Piles heap
on the outskirts. The outskirts

creep. An orchard could be
in the light at the end of the open hangar.
I cannot see to the edge.

I copy what the dead sang
about the fangs of the wind
though the wind has been defanged.

The piles. The outskirts.
I creep. I sleep.

Reliance Inventory

Extractor by birth, receiver
by nettle petal north of west huzzah buzz

I crumbled the phallus carved into the sea cliff
listened as wind

etched in the pale palimpsest its flyleaf of *A Thousand Sleeps.*

Gray whale boomed, I ran down
the cliff to follow its northbound booming,
feet drumming the packed sand until I had neither

Domestic Tranquility nor The Blessings of Liberty,
the power to coin money, nor to provide and maintain a navy,

and hid my ribs
on the pale underside of a fern.

There dreamed on fins
the milk-torch passing through eons,

woke and spied on the Fathers weeping their Leviathan
had washed up on shore, soggy pulp
picked at by beaks

of others,
tagged and collared

herring gull   American shad   *pinus contorta*
agate   immigrant

blamed for blunt-sparking dry fir needles
(it was white teens with matches

from pornographic matchbox torturing grasshoppers after masturbating).
Old-growth smoke   climax-particles in   alveoli
I get so low

I have to rest every ten steps under
the ash-blackened glacier—
could it be even in these moments melting audibly faster?—

where the broadleaf lupine with its fuzzy pods, little pea-purses
packed with enzyme inhibitors does not long sustain

the fantasy one could graze
placidly upon the summer-abandoned ski run blazed purple by it
if one's little bags of California

dates, walnuts, petered out.
I only had to eat two of the raspberry cannabis gummies
I carried with me

to see the stacked cairns
guiding me across countless snowmelt gorges,
across fields of black volcanic powder to my waiting car

worn down to powder and blown away.

Users with Access

Access roads crush their gravels over
        "a mountain where spirits dwell
        "a spring of ceremonial water

Gate code is 1830
        1876 also works
                1890, 1973

"9 out of 10 better dead" to paraphrase
the big stick face carved into the mountain

Heirs have redrawn the district
to include more cottonwoods and junipers
        "It's their own fault for not voting"

Leaf-buds   museum prayer beads   eternity
will run out of money in 2019
                        without more pumps

Put on your mask of instrument panel light,
crack Dakota Kid seeds to stay awake,
        piss in a Big Gulp, toss it in a ditch

Prometheus's descendant
hides in the Killdeer Mountains,
crushed rig hand turned populist
                liquor picks his liver daily

gas flares   gas flares   gas flares
        illuminate the canyonland

"We know the Indians
got a bad deal, we watch *Bonanza*

in the afternoon. She doesn't need
our permission to marry him"

"You can go anywhere,
even off the marked trails"

     Like that, I am the first person

to sign in at the box since November,

walk down into the canyon familiar
from the window of the long drives
from my own through my parents' childhoods

My father young near here
                    carried a long icicle
containing all the world's light
home from his route, a little late,
     his father smashed it rightfully against the house

The icicle is whole, doesn't melt, I am
pierced in a dream and no one can tell
I go on in pangs trying to conceal it

rightfully rightfully to the face
in the mountain streaked
     by petrochemical rains,

its burning immobile lips somehow speaking
in the voice of my father's father, saying

"Nothing ever tasted better
     than snowmelt in the canyon trickling
under the bed
of a washed-out road I was repairing"

Stranded at Alpha

Your neighbor does alpha
exercises on his wolves:

tall as deer,
glacial eyes.

His fences crackle.

On this mountain he grows
marijuana and wolves.

Like everyone else up here, you say,
he is mere receiver

for the satellites you pick
like shells from the night sky's shores

to listen down the long winding futures.

You only mention him
because in this exercise he has created

he is alpha.

*

If we could arrive where we are, I think,
the grid of twine fastened to stakes and
the vines' crazing would clarify

afternoon's aslant
like a damper pedal slowly lifted.

But strung from end to end of the valley below us
the cables' dominant chord buzzes:

power without face,
force without difficulty.

We stare only
at two lights, you say: fire and screens.

You touch and touch a screen.

*

Smell of ash in the stove: it is morning.
We wake on a firebreak road
no fire climbs to.

You touch
the fine hairs of the apricots
where cold sunlight touches.

It's as if they are a little beyond
where sunlight touches.

It's as if at a threshold
you've knocked

and not been let in.

*

The workmen cut down the daffodils
lighting the doorway of your shack.

Inconsolable, you left your love back there
to tell me another woman

wants to fly you to Trieste, Odessa, anywhere,
perhaps one day pay for your cryonics.

But for years you've disciplined your love's
art; loosed to another she might have babies, write
about babies, mere
human babies.

A dog has followed us three days
to this promontory; you let it lick your hand,
compassionate.

*

Camera batteries in dust
high above Silicon Valley:

it's all captured   it won't get away.

I pick up a fragment of clay, ancient-
seeming, mechanically
stamped: "Bio . . ."

We'll escape, you think, the wedding of life and death
just as the last amphorae are emptied.

You are writing a novel
about a man on a mountain
who suspects everyone below is dead.

He engineers children
with his DNA, instructs them
to long to resurrect him someday . . .

I go off alone,
unable, even, to find my way back

to that sunrise grotto
where a cat flicks a mosquito from its ear

in my journal.

TWO

Arrival at the Complex

Over the rutted high road of this
            preserve, wide white
contrails converge, dimensioning
            a cloudless vast wash
above snow-battened grass: crisscross stalks,

some pressed, some melt-released, conduct acute
            sun-slant down tangent
            conduits—pattern
            circumscribed like
Potawatomi basketwork in a museum by
            four roads' roar,
            township, county,
            principality, continually
appearing in satellite photographs, proving here

is a gray rectangle of hectares containing
            two kidney-shaped lakes
            adjacent the new
tech park, commissioned to manufacture hope
            in this corner of the one
state so beleaguered it lost citizens
            in the last census. Gone
from the oaks that line the road across the upper prairie

are the thick leaves that hid the monolithic
            fabrication plant
from sight all fall: here it is, one unbroken shape, ugly as any
            surface without complexity
at every level of scale must be to us
whose deepest pathways are in-nested whorls, in-
            comprehensible
tessellations of intervolving spirals, branches, nebulae, yet

this complex, I
    guess, conceals
intricacies obscure to me, that underwrite
    the flour of the very
bread in me, the synthetic fiber
of the fleece that holds my heat from
    January cold,
the corrective, shatterproof, and double-
paned glass that moves me through and keeps me.

Winter Asylum

Off the path: the demolished
        hospital's littered ravine.
Single yellow bricks
stamped: Standard Steel, West Branch.
      Broken plates, the bottom
           of a mug. Jars, jars, jars,
like larvae emerging from mud—
           thaw softened them free—I can see
in a week great
           industrial moths blacken the sky.
But these are duds
opaque as blown light bulbs,
           the broken packed with earth—
           earthdark footlights
to a rifled display of brown, outmoded, standardized
shoes—
        some with stitches softened loose, tongues
                pulled free—
              a gag reflex
takes the ravine.
I am its depressor,
        who could as easily lift
                from this tumbled,
                amputated turntable
                a thunderous

Freude!
a tide
       across the blood-brain barrier
        like that tide contained once in these un-stopped
brown glass bottles, narrow, buried
       in one deep cache—
                music, *medication time.*
                The actress playing the nurse
                dispenses pills.

Nothing monstrous darkens the sky, yet I can't escape

that scene, or the language
that has come to make everything—trees, clouds, frozen lakes
                              its instrument
of self-correction. I am tripped up by
                              these severed ends

of an ancient wire fence hidden under
a felt of leaves:
                    the fences are down.
                    Asylum is everywhere.

Constructing a Center

A sign: "Asylum Lake, a nature preserve owned
by Westward Push University,"
among whose collections one might find many copies

>   of Rousseau: *you are lost*
>   *if you forget that the fruits of the earth belong*
>   *to all and the earth to no one,*

he says, who is lost
among binaries, classifications,
a projection

>   of a holographic primitive
>   our nostalgia passes through without resistance
>   like signals through miles of fiber optics.

I might have said—but who am I?—*through unboundaried zones*
of tallgrass prairie, lowland marsh, transitional
hardwood, suggesting an inhabitable distance

>   between a self at any instant
>   and its unassimilables—
>   this stand of oaks, for instance, depicted beside itself

on a tacked-up digitized map that makes it contiguous
with quadrants covering Earth. It belongs to all
in the bared redundancy of its patterns—

>   they may be analyzed, filed
>   among the established
>   laws—biodiversity, entropy,

repetition compulsion. My returning today
after two weeks' hiatus to find a new way
from the same parking lot starting point

        is likely diagnosable; yet, I begin again
        at the west entry, walking the upper prairie
        along the oaks' edge and an edge of

tall dried yellow grass standing aslant, until I am stopped
at the sight of this anomaly: one young oak
growing across the border of the road, barely

        taller than the surrounding grass.
        In the fork of its lowest branch,
        this difference:

against entropy
this tiny intricacy holding fast: a nest
lined with downy tessellated feathers,

        whose outer convex weave is
        three kinds of grass and tiny unlikely
        elm leaves, gathered to integrity

over countless branch-spans,
grass-patches, however distance is lived
unmeasured, from within, constructing a center

        of that lived distance—new, and of startling
        ingenuity: a type of thread-thin stem or twig,
        some available particle, affix, sewn tightly

into an enclosing rim, as text marks may
by solemn painstaking displace us
into the widest strangeness of a place.

Tracing the Grooves

Housebound two days
               in storm, going round and round
the cheap used
               vinyl of a Bach fugue,
until it turns merely
ecclesiastical, and I no longer feel it
                              as *a lament*
for the transitory nature of the worldly.

Deep roads
       reach Asylum
Lake. Snow
is flying parallel
       the flattened grass
so fast it seems   not to fall, seems
a great ragged flag of surrender flying.

Into drifts, under branches piled white,
I walk into a clearing where
                      snow slows,
and in sunbreak sifts
       like that "snow"
                of diatoms

onto the slopes of submarine mountains
taller than terrestrial mountains, which, so long
as sea surrounds them,
       will never erode. The worldly is more
multiple than Bach's unshattered
mirror showed.

A ghost-branch of heavy snow
                falls from an oak branch.
Years ago a storm-snapped branch fell
and shattered my dear friend's skull.

These oaks creak
with white weight,
                              like doors
that could blow open any moment
on an otherworld
                without *because*, without
                conjunction at all.

My friend is in me
on this mountain too deep
to see again. We had crept to the edge
                of a thousand-foot plummet
                in the Cascades.
He is stuck
                on that ridge,
looking down,
his face
                a blank lit by abyss.

A branch like a stylus fell

        onto that silence whose
        grooves, groves
        now everywhere turn

                under no sun, no moon.

All Forks

I take the lake fork today:
              grass gives way to
saplings, bushes, vines,
              every type
              of branching thing. My eye
              picks a red-barked
       bush from the field's edge:
       forks in threes radiate
       around the red
       main stem,
       but
symmetry
       eludes me:
              up through
              their flexible predilections
              these
              forks radiate
in relation to every other fork-
              in-the-field's sun-seeking,
       raising a staggering
       dynamism
of caught
droplet lights. The ways one eye could trace
              from fork to fork
       across the field balk
       calculation. Still, I long
to take all forks at once,
              to find a formula by which
upper prairie, frozen marsh, dry creek bed might
       condense to an infinitesimal
              equilibrium of
              deep structure
              and surface
              tension, yet

one touch
of this red branch and beads slide
         into beads,
         shiver free, re-
         coalesce at new
                        coordinates
                        on the bush.
The way is newly
lighted as

the iced-over snowed-over lake in cloudbreak is
         brilliant, and, ice melted,
                        under cloud, is
                                   dull,

so that the number of forks must be multiplied by
         the number of days, hours, less—
and to take each way in each

combination, even in this meager preserve,
would take more attention than many lifetimes contain.

What a choice, then,
to walk this moment this brilliant
edge

of lake and sky.

February Twenty-Ninth

Earth's extra
        yearly quarter-turn
brings me here:
                        the first of Actual, unseasonable
warmth, expansion
                        of hard-hearted ground
                        to mud and mist, of my loosening
joints to loping
        downhill through soft leaf duff and decompositions to
the thawing edge of
                        song: lapping
free from stiffened reeds,
                        absorbing the long frozen
                designations
                        into its motions—
a mush of footprints melting
                to nourish the hidden
seeds:
        cotyledons soon
                        will crack the million acorns open—
earth make room!

I hear over the hill
                        cries of children, nascent
        season adventing
its difference in this,
                        see a cloven print in mud, a pyramid
of shining black droppings hinting. I follow

the lake road,
smell the very pebbles underfoot, the clay,
a resurrected sense
                of self long dormant, inspiring
                leaves' outgassing, ice's subliming,

corresponding with
beauty, illusory,
               needful: the very first
mosquito's lacy flight
among brush: called again to world's-blood,
                         the circulations
continue! Sunfish
          hunkered
             in bottom-mud beat
free, cruise the new
rotunda of green columns sunlight is
erecting in lake water through
                 apertures in ice,
and I scuttle through these rapidly renewing
ruins—
oak canopies anticipating with hard leaf buds
             Earth's coming inclination, sun's
influence finding
        its trillion fulfillments: long strands
of moss sway
on the lake bottom, the white swan glides into its procreative cove
along a gap thawed in ice,
     and in its awakened wake,
water-striders test their oars again,
cloud-slow, on this cloud-reflecting
road,

and it must be this hour is not beholden
to any calendar's benumbed march
of days because

I am outside and shedding my heavy coat!

Riddled Territory

March tenth, record heat. A too-positive
arctic oscillation
      trapped cold north. Everywhere early
bees cruise—incredulous,
            I project.
Pollen collects
on hoods of cars. The radio fears
    a last frost
    will sear
leaves, kill crops, or,
      apples, cherries, won't get the night cool
needed to ripen. Cruel how it seems

there are incalculable ways to inhabit
          airy contingency,
and almost no place to be

      beyond the designated
          frequencies.
I come close today
      to a hawk's dark
silhouette in the single tree on the grass's edge—
it falls
    to flight, broadcasting
    its shadow across
    the grass-roof, into the root-dens
of rodents—doubtless

stopping them in adrenaline freeze—
    and glides to watchful rest on a branch beyond
Asylum's edge.

A rumored shadow, I think, is our habitual
       dread: talk
of the Palisades Reactor at Covert downgraded,
of possible meltdown,
             risk-benefit, profit—
             a hawk

on the screen in every pocket, our stress-response
             so subtle-constant it lies
             just below the threshold of sense.

I had hoped (warily) something unscripted
here would release me
                into its urgency,

but the redwing clicks now
like a lighter struggling to finally ignite,
the cardinal echoes with *drop drop drop drop drop*—like
             beads of gasoline
             falling into this dry holographic
fire of purple floral tangles
       that sends up its chemical lavender scent,
and everywhere is downwind

of human diminishment. At last, I think,
I have proven these walks
                a failure
to dwell upon Earth.
I can excuse myself

from the territory: Asylum
referring only to referring.
             Absolved from caring,

I take the central hill road back,
pause for the first time at
             two weathered wooden birdhouses

beneath a single hill-tree,
see hovering
in the hole of one a delicate wasp, see fallen

       beneath the other a square
       cake of grass frosted
       with gray feathers,
       a nest

I turn over to find it
          thick with ants
seething to purposes irretrievably beyond

the riddle of *last*.

Coda: Spring

Took the usual path
the other direction   half-hollowed

oak trunk ringed
                with white half-moon mushrooms held up
one leaf-budded branch in
mist. Went among the least

changes possible to notice,
          to be in other words

what I am regardless of words.
On a screen of new-green forest one ridge tree in full
whiteflower. I

whiteflower
        with each shout
from the school group's sinuous line below me

that mimics the meadow creek's insouciant crayon-line path
through high grass.
                  I'd forgotten how
to let hand,
        body, boots, gallop
                in front of intention,
to leave hindsight like a kite caught
in lines
        others left on the sky, to leave
foresight's leveled forests standing awhile and not

for the old Romantic lie
        memory of it will make livable the tedium
of a city's rooms,

but because through this web hung now
        high in canopy-light

this sun-struck eye-lessness, I
dilates.

THREE

Rude Mechanical

The driven-past child
will forget my face
                    like the spring-

creek, where in grass it bends
           through the throughscape,

the brook trout holding
on its back the seasons streaming

precedes itself and blue
has no relation to

           the white-houred
           the burst-haired

sweetness-machine of the blackberry flower

the without-scope that escaped
the I   I was those miles

of brittle certainty   likeness-machine
habitually solving

sun setting in gaps of a passing train,
a season's sap rising in steam from a sugar shack,
oak leaves blown over a graveyard wall,

those flashes

           not an answer to any question

Wrecked Eclogue

Ring of wasps, black sticky
ring of fallen pears
this side the ruined wall

The other side a rich country
debates its carrying capacity

I have felt in certain houses mostly lost
the architect considered sun's path
along sky there

Memory, cold warmth,
afternoon in another room

Music lights up the lost
bookstore by the sea,
its cats curling the shelves dead

Her old letters seem
written to the oddling I've become:
"leaf-lace   aphids' graces
squash flower un-insulted
Gunday morning"   In glimpses

a fox goes by
red-blonde as red-blonde
tallgrass, it crosses
the highway as the field
will one day on
an afternoon in another room

A child, I scratched from dirt
the tiny key furred with corrosion
it opened in me
this ivy canticle climbing invasively

Adult, please don't promise
love or sanctum, promise never
to make scarcity of abundance

I promise the iridescent
round plates behind a toad's eyes
shimmering audition, and—
seed-sized nostrils poised
above the water-line—
calm immersion in quickgold afternoon

in another room
tan of a cliff after its petroglyphs
were blasted for a train to pass

I saw and said I will write
a song impossible to cover
because recorded by spiny burrs
fallen in haphazards

When you see me seated facing away
from the viewpoint, know me
caretaker of what was lost already when entrusted

Now Under Wind Take

Saw fossil
reef from when

      underwater,
      this ridge

Now under wind
take
      my child-hand

I don't give
to just anybody
      what I no longer have

Streams, you
said,
bump nuts along

      At a creeping pace
we can't match
    hickories walk
      up-valley

It's not love
I feel
it's

sunset colors on a cliff face
before history

Walks Scribbled over Scribbled over Walks

Cold hole in my right pant
through which
                    grass's eyelash brushes my calf,

flirty infinite

*

I'm shimmery, holographic,
mental projection on a stone church floor labyrinth

by a bored peasant
in a lost epoch
                    John Clodpebble
his knack

not for conjuring face-shapes in clouds (commonplace)
but cloud-shapes in faces (wow)

                    I'm Son of Clod,
glimpse in a passing face

          burn scars on the sand where the reenactment was filmed

*

I've without even grinding by crawling across continents
my body down found
                    the grail Américain:

dry cob in dust, rusty where chewed,
roughish, weighty, OK lob it into

stalks stalks

      ritual?
      yes, unrepeatable

Its arc etches sky with the shell pattern rumored lost

*

Off-trail uphill
snagged and snagged by thorns until
a deer-thoroughfare opens, then:

      a burr on the haunch
      of a cloud, I float around . . .

nary a highwayman!
                tra-la

    I can even pretend

cyber-warriors aren't hunting me in the wireless air

*

Remember Grasmere Gulch?
O subdivided Youth!

I caught Chinook smolts in the big river,

sneaked them in plastic bag plumped with water
past the treatment hut,

      poured them out in the creeklet pool
where it burped from its pipe, waited

for the flickers of life,
but

three years later
got my license and had better things to do

than check if any returned from sea

*

I long to let walking be

about the great not-me, but

here's a refrigerator wrecked in a ravine

        and I remember: 8, anxiously awake
at midnight, I was

discovered at the kitchen table
        drawing plans

for the power plant run
by house-sized magnets of opposite polarity

and urged to go back to sleep

*

My legs by their gear-grinding
whir me open   dada contraption
in love with its uselessness

                (eggbeater-cloudbeater)

*

I, Clodpebble the Nth, admit
I was trying to have an experience

So, the bridge in the city of jazz leads to
a gateless hinge pitted by rust on a post in a field,

I guess there's nothing left to open

              and, as teens with stones
must naturally smash

old plate-glass windows in an abandoned factory,
I smashed the creek ice into tangent panels
with the stick I carry,

was thrilled the next day by
the layered way the fragments had re-frozen

*

What is not information?

(riddle)

my religion's only sacred text

if I had a religion

I'd text it to you

if I had your number

*

I admit I have a religion,
THE DOCTRINE AND, and
                      it changes hourly:

now it is a road curving uphill out of sight,
now a bloody feather

I'm not, however,
going to try to fly off into the "circumambient gases"
or tickle infinity, I'll just hunker
          in mud and mend this schism

between the bird imagery faction
          (who prefer the riddle of the whole sky contained
          in an acorn-sized speckled egg)

and the fish imagery sect
          (who say a hundred fingerlings breaking the surface at once
          escaping some larger thing
          ought to be stamped in metal somehow
          on wind-chimes and hung in our yards)

Sure, I say, and
          a farm dog tugging with bared teeth at a deer corpse in a ditch
          could be nice in gold stitching
          and a child breathing between gulps of water from a cup
          could be Hymn no. 2 in the Hymn Book

What about Hymn no. 1?
It would be confusing to have one
in this religion: the congregants are clouds and me
strip by strip peeling
a stick to arrive again at fingertip idiot joy

Don't peace me when I'm in this state!

Your hair will get bark flakes all in it
and your hair is so nuanced and sculpted right now
you look like the antipope
my religion would hire if we could afford it

Will you be our antipope, pro bono, bro?

All you've got to do is walk around looking
like whatever happens next is not

the very thing

Two Notes

walking stick propped
against porch rail,
vine-circled to the top

*

pings and pings
fabrication plant
            synonyms
for lying gnat-dance

            Peace Walker smelled
river water wick stiff stems, saw
            a pony bolt
                        in sharp delight

I've gone far
            digging out a vine
    roots entangling
a single note
                        buried chime

bullet-heavy packed with dirt,
holding it,
            listening to wind

Sick Georgic

Having neither flock nor hill, forgive me,
I imitate what I do not understand.

The loose tarps rip against themselves in wind.
A grass-overgrown trough is what's left
of the palace complexes.

A dog licks from a drain by votives
still flickering the next morning.

The old man's face suspends there
as the younger lifts up the match:
like that moment when, driving by them,

the rows of stalks go suddenly parallel.

*

Reclamation by drainage reveals
the necropolis. Earrings shimmer
next to brown skulls emerging from mud,

bringing down the angel Curation.

I wear the mark of gold burrs on rolled cuffs,
escape along the dry watercourses

to that square not yet remembered for tears falling
from the tip of the nose onto the touchscreen.

*

Hail on the empty terrace.
A stripped bicycle chained to a lamppost.

Having neither hut nor pond, let's stay
in this room and cultivate gentleness.

Machines will do the sorting and remembering.
Machines will run the kidneys and the lottery,
insert the repeat lines in their places:

No one can take your loneliness.

*

Read of the monumental eros
of the dead, read
the wildflower identification book all winter.

She held a dripping sponge
in the doorway, saying goodbye.

A bottle fell from a drunk's pack, didn't break.

"Imagine you are guarded by chance."

It was like a dream of rain falling
into an unfinished cathedral
to one from a country of extractable minerals.

*

To find what heroes missed,
I wander not far.

The river squeezes through
the broken locks. Wanderers toss dice
against the cracked abutments.
My secrets are not different
from the secrets of the others:

It's easier to pile rocks than watch a cloud very long.
Taught to solve for x, but not to taste food.
Taught by the older children

to throw sharp stones at slow-dying spawning
black salmon.

To find what heroes missed, I sit watching the river
compelled to leap its hurdles endlessly.

*

Stars over gravel
a cat sunned on earlier,
your your

is as first raindrops
on paving stones, as

cloud-break sunlight
through a train window shows
the fiery transparency
of a sleeping child's eyelids.

No one can take your loneliness.

*

I admire that emperor,
I forget which,

who, asked to return
from a far province to the throne, demurred,
"I'd rather stay here and grow cabbages."

But having neither plot nor packet
of dragon's teeth, Pythagorean
past lives nor opinion

why sea shells are found sometimes
on the slopes of peaks, I merely imitate

what I do not intend
to improve upon, whatever rough

or folded shows the impetus written into it
against entropy:

the cut cabbage cascading through itself,
the vertiginous rude crag
intended as mere background to the conversion scene,

whose knotty stylization kept me a long time in that gallery.

FOUR

In the Shadow of the Reactor

God of Grids,
hear my attention.

Winged seeds spin down
into counter-
spinning
eddies,

likeness fled
awe-soon.

Show me a battery as yet
can store it,
awe.

From the dry riverbed of this
language's end,
what was
maple

rises utterly.

Litany

I am with you where no preference is
Sunlight climbs the nail
I am a with a with   not a you
where the ice has gone

Two planes fly over
a deer skeleton dug up
I am with you where no preference is   la la

A book of light crosses
the forest floor   I cannot
read in receptors all down my length   nevertheless

I am a with
the blue absolutely
through the pales of the corn rattles inaugurates

Flattened vole,
the stair metaphor has taken the schools,
a nut rebounds from a stone
as if a great caution about occurrences suddenly
was not

and I was a with   held
in the swept pile of the hair of many heads
the hair of the stem of the coneflower
of the beardtongue

speaking nevertheless
no preference be with you   as I am

by a stream that doesn't even keep
any course or calendar
listening to its un-listening

I learned it on this pilgrimage to the Middle
from two great ones who looked up from the ribs
of the owl they were eating, I learned to be a with, largely

the rooms in any glance   you can't go in

Marshy ravine your one week of unprepossessing raggy rustishness
like lit storefronts dark closes down around
the instruments searching out conditions miss

like a friend's face
in the face of an ancient
statue brought up from the bottom of a lake
the museum's closed-circuit cameras are closed to

like scent of winter's broken branches sawn in segments
warming in the sun welcome as

one who greeted us tenderly in childhood
with the unplanned obsolescence of all
rains

Rain turning to snow across the stadium lights be with you
"Rifle-Range Impact Area" on a fence of tangled purples be with
you data collectors banding kestrels ankles be with
you lineup of planes hanging over the dusk-colored lake be with
you emptiness that displaces very water

One Unlearning

The beetle wing startled
in me all
my kingdom for no kingdom

Vine leaves over hills waved
neither hello nor good-
anything

waved selfsame
to one unlearning

the inches gathering rain
the kinds of the lightning

Sieve

Stolen *selahs* and orchard
steeps, hourless flowers
of our grafted speech, this rest
before the branch becomes
instrument is infinite
decimals to reach one reached
in one nakedness, is the you not yours
to give you give
as hail-dimpled sand
vanishes through a starry sieve

Havening

We are each
other's not safe.

Breath is you slip
from the image

of you. The pulse
at your neck

is shocking.
Touches my

touched eyes.
You

of the
roe-small,

freckler
of vacancy.

Be given,
not partial;

the world is
no-sided.

Unfastening

As a cicada pupa nails its clawed shell to a post
and, winged, escapes itself, we clawed
and left our bodies on the bed.

Fell back, feet in the comforter's cold
lake-bottom muck,
debris around our eyes at the waterline.

A walnut fruit thudded the roof
and instantly countless roots held the house up.

Roll over. What does it fasten
if we pull? The long
silts filter. The blinds go

the color of sleep in a raft,
and I complain beauty is
a book-word now like *undreggy,*

but you know better, or feel better, rather,
remembering the one

who laid his small all, his full
human length down on a dry road before rain

to leave a figure he
could stand to see
disappearing.

Interjection

You caryatids,
dried-hive-heads shadowing

the infant's nails, eyelashes,
every of-its-own-accord-
formed-perfectly thing,

you dead
who carried the words to our mouths
when no one asked

interjecting
these dials the sun still circles,

you watch
from the words the fallen leaves catch rain as if
still waiting

for some identification.

Coat

Far snag, small turtle
brushing flies from its face

You unshelled—
your hair floats strangely
in your child-bath bodily trance

Put on your coat, let's go
again among snakes and turtles, oaks, the us
there's no pronoun for

Your coat, someday, a doll's coat
in a box I open   I close again   give away
this day that day

Ah, son, what my own father could not explain
for all he tried—

your coat

Aftercast

She would recall aspen-silver winds
on the river ridge   giving birth to him

My son my suddenly

Imagine a
mosquito having a name

"I've been hiding the hurt part,
the part that's most alive . . ."

Under the bridge a woman peels
a massive root on the overturned bottom of a box
A man sits next to her with his shirt off

My suddenly   my grown son

the strangeness of having known
anyone

a cloud flashes
through a pooled tire-tread

Reed

Fire-banked color
of oak leaves after
a season under snow:

> mask of light
> on every your face.

Here is a reed.
        Take what spoke
what ancients spoke.

What goes filling in
these claw-marks in mud with impossible gear teeth,
ice?

It's turning us.
Here is a road.

On either side, you of many eras,

your eyes wasps' empty papery hexagons,
your eyes asterisks
of ice.

Take this reed down that road.

In the Preserve

Blinds of the half-demolished building blew openly.

I entered through the arch lit by sere leaves.

Lightning flashed in the icicles.

C played the *Pathétique* unfamiliar.

I lay on the rectangle of our collective imagining.

Against the canceled vastness.

Come back to this season if you can get past Hope.

See lead from Roman forges in bubbles in arctic ice.

An alien oak under a cat's cradle of cables.

Where ditch and river meet.

Some breakthroughs of sun flashing the panels.

Loneliness of woodsmoke and a radio.

Rain when you fell asleep, snow when you woke.

C said it was like visiting another country.

Mounds of frozen waves brought the horizon close.

The creek trickled through the canted slabs.

As sunlight resists us somewhat.

I ripped the leatherette cover from a journal given to me.

Admired the dried glue swirled unselfconsciously by hand.

Deep melt in the ditch-pond doubled sunset.

A swallow gathered beyonds on a peeled branch.

Each thing presented itself out of all of its seasons.

Snow crumbled like yellow flecks of glue from an old binding.

Thick brush broke open a shack and let sky in.

The river sieved through a metal shopping cart.

That was the bottom of the dream.

C said we live no other.

A pocket of snowflakes changed direction like a school of herring.

Snow is falling missed more motions than I could make it mean.

The fool only gives the others back to themselves.

A scarecrow, chrome globe for a head.

Seven stories of casino parking by the filtration plant.

Thirty trailers of coarse salt.

Cell phone birdsong with its one meaning.

Everything you see is paid for.

The guru breathing into the microphone after it's over.

Thoreau attributed to Hawthorne.

A hat-less acorn.

Frost like dominoes on the same side of every stem.

A law there's no following.

I followed an oak-leaf's footprint across new snow.

Found a windy dune like a struck tuning fork haloing itself.

Went to gather alone to bring to C.

She was everywhere like cloudshadow bending the grasses.

Unverifiable and utterly.

Out of the vastness without trespass.

A glacial tone, a cloud-and-water surround.

A boarded-up school holding open echoes.

A blue flame under a teakettle hovering on a branch in a window.

The prisoner of war picnic shelter empty at that hour.

Snow falling through streetlights and headlights.

What any evening I may come out and have all to myself.

A motion sensor tripped by lichen dilating in moonlight.

What any morning I may come out and have all to myself.

Different birdsong on either side of the house.

Simplicity Patterns on a factory freaked with vines.

Pieces of hail striking the cable, bouncing off in loopy trajectories.

Gulls resting on the pond-ice's melt-margin.

Huge old oaks following a lost road through thin new growth.

A snarl of grass and twigs where something lives under the eaves.

In the House of Long Views.

Listened to the *Om* of the refrigerator.

From a window watched screens flashing in other windows.

Sun rose from a chimney.

Ago crept like cloudshadow o'er.

A daughter led her daughter through the falling flakes across.

Gentleness as much.

I brought it when I could.

I brought whatever had fallen across my path.

The creek's lights guttering.

Liquor bottles and wrappers of a rabbit's habitat.

A man shoveling, his dog leaping to meet the leaping snow.

Motions not me that became me.

A man stood in a doorway watching until a woman drove away.

The bones dissolve on their own in the gold cans.

An agreement made on our behalf.

C said we could get away with watching the heron that close to the plant.

I said it was like visiting another country.

Attention being of a kind.

Being without kind or degree.

No way to say it utterly.

The rain has dash the rain has down.

A snail is safe from hail.

Purple yellow.

Sugar maples stand as if they revolved around the sun.

C welcomes me at January's door.

In the silence of cars passing and a far helicopter.

A swallow drinking melt out in the namelessness.

Notes

Page 13: The open quotes at the beginning of "Users with Access" are adapted from the article "The misguided archaeological review behind the Dakota Access Pipeline," by Chip Colwell, in the *Colorado Independent,* November 25, 2016.

Page 19: Poems in section two are drawn from notes scribbled after walks taken two to three times weekly from January through April 2012 in the Asylum Lake preserve in Kalamazoo, Michigan.

Page 25: The Rousseau quote is from "Discourse on the Origin and Basis of Inequality among Men."

Page 27: "Tracing the Grooves" is dedicated to the memory of Patrick Duff.

Page 49: "circumambient gases" is from "Romanticism and Classicism" by T. E. Hulme.

Page 54: The emperor is Diocletian. From Gibbon's *Decline and Fall of the Roman Empire,* chapter 13: "His answer to Maximian is deservedly celebrated. He was solicited by that restless old man to reassume the reins of government, and the Imperial purple. He rejected the temptation with a smile of pity, calmly observing, that if he could show Maximian the cabbages which he had planted with his own hands at Salona, he should no longer be urged to relinquish the enjoyment of happiness for the pursuit of power."

Acknowledgments

Bomb (online): "In the Preserve," "Litany," "Unfastening"

Bombay Gin: "Aftercast"

The Carolina Quarterly: "Riddled Territory"

Conjunctions (Online Exclusive): "Stranded at Alpha," "Walks Scribbled over Scribbled over Walks"

Crazyhorse: "Havening"

Cream City Review: "Interjection"

Diagram: "Magnifier," "In Case of Loss," "Reliance Inventory," "Users with Access"

Diode Poetry Journal: "All Forks"

Field: "Coat," "Reed"

The Journal: "The Lover in Winter Plaineth"

Notre Dame Review: "Two Notes"

Portland Review: "Arrival at the Complex," "Tracing the Grooves"

Rhino: "Comedy of Mirrors"

Salamander: "Winter Asylum"

Water~Stone Review: "February Twenty-Ninth"

West Branch: "One Unlearning," "Sieve"

Witness: "In the Shadow of the Reactor," "Sick Georgic"

The author is grateful to the Ragdale Foundation for a residency in which some of these poems were written, and to *Rhino* for awarding its 2014 Editors' Prize to "Comedy of Mirrors."

Deep gratitude to Kazim Ali for choosing *Magnifier* for the Colorado Prize, to Laura Mackin and George Porteus for their cover illustration that brilliantly evokes the spirit of these poems, and to Stephanie G'Schwind and the Center for Literary Publishing for designing a beautiful book;

to Bill Olsen and Nancy Eimers, whose insight and encouragement helped shape this book; to Nic Witschi for mentorship and, with Jeffrey Angles, for generous readings of an early draft; and to Richard Kenney, Heather McHugh, and Roger Gilbert for the lasting influence of their teaching;

to friends whose talk and work has been sustaining: Glenn Shaheen, Laurie Cedilnik, Elizabyth Hiscox, Douglas Jones, Andrew Weissenborn, Scott Bade, Franklin K. R. Cline, Olivia Clare, T. Zachary Cotler, Michael Rutherglen, David Welch, Pattabi Seshadri, Alex Walton, Avery Slater, Steve Dold, Lacey Henson, Sean Clemmons, Kevin Craft, Katie Ogle, Sierra Nelson, Rebecca Hoogs, Johnny Horton, Will Bernhard, Carol Light, Joshua Beckman, Matt Dube, Stephanie Carpenter, Emily Robbins, Jeff Allen, Jeff Voccola, Andy Vogel, and Cherri Buijk;

and to my family for their love and support, especially to Colleen for cultivating a shared writing life with me and for so much more, and to Ezra, our joy.

This book is set in Sabon
by the Center for Literary Publishing
at Colorado State University.

Copyediting by Geneva McCarthy.
Proofreading by Daniel Schonning.
Book design and typesetting by Michelle LaCrosse.
Cover design by Stephanie G'Schwind.
Cover artwork by Laura Mackin and George Porteus.
Printing by BookMobile.